People Who

Written by Catherine Baker

Collins

2

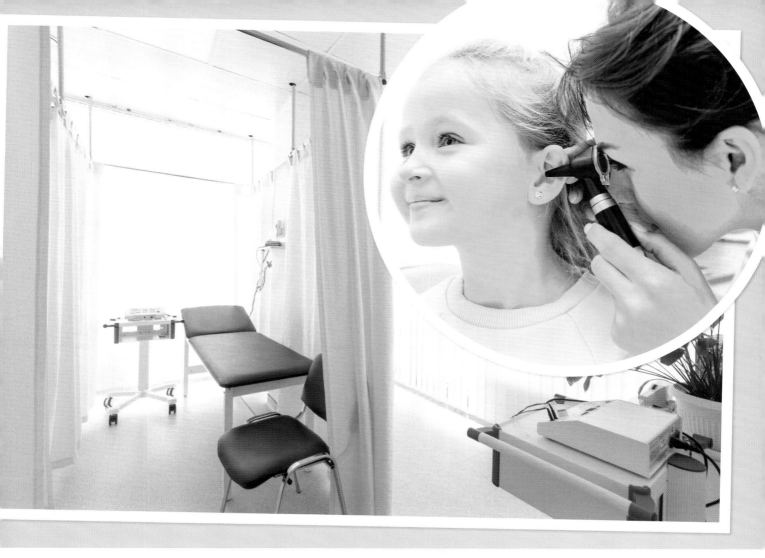

Who helps us?

 Review: After reading

Read 1: Decoding

- Look for and discuss the items in the small circles at the bottom of the pages (what noise do they make, if any?). Try to copy some of the noises using voice sounds and body percussion.
- Talk about the soft and loud noises they might hear if they were in the scene. (e.g. *sirens, crackle of fire*; *school bell ringing, sound of children reading and writing*)
- Look for opportunities to explore alliteration, by focusing on things in the pictures that begin with /h/ or /f/ on pages 2–3, /b/ on pages 4–5, /ch/ on pages 6–7, /p/ on pages 8–9, /t/ on pages 10–11, and /l/ on pages 12–13.

Read 2: Prosody

- Encourage the children to hold the book and turn the pages.
- Spend time looking at the photos and discussing them, drawing on any relevant experience or knowledge the children have. Encourage them to talk about what is happening in each picture, giving as much detail as they can.

Read 3: Comprehension

- Look at pages 14 and 15 together and ask the children to look out for people helping each other.
- For every question ask the children how they know the answer. Ask:
  - Do you have a lollipop person to help you when you come to school? How do you get to school? Do you think lollipop people are helpful?
  - How do police officers help us? (e.g. *giving directions/helping lost children/stopping crime/ keeping people safe*)